KS2
8–9
Years

G000299552

Master Maths at Home

Fractions and Decimals

Scan the QR code to help your child's learning at home.

 | **MATHS** **NO PROBLEM!**

How to use this book

Maths — No Problem! created **Master Maths at Home** to help children develop fluency in the subject and a rich understanding of core concepts.

Key features of the Master Maths at Home books include:

- Carefully designed lessons that provide structure, but also allow flexibility in how they're used.

- Speech bubbles containing content designed to spark diverse conversations, with many discussion points that don't have obvious 'right' or 'wrong' answers.

- Rich illustrations that will guide children to a discussion of shapes and units of measurement, allowing them to make connections to the wider world around them.

- Exercises that allow a flexible approach and can be adapted to suit any child's cognitive or functional ability.

- Clearly laid-out pages that encourage children to practise a range of higher-order skills.

- A community of friendly and relatable characters who introduce each lesson and come along as your child progresses through the series.

You can see more guidance on how to use these books at **mastermathsathome.com**.

We're excited to share all the ways you can learn maths!

Maths — No Problem!
mastermathsathome.com
www.mathsnoproblem.com
hello@mathsnoproblem.com

First published in Great Britain in 2022 by
Dorling Kindersley Limited
One Embassy Gardens, 8 Viaduct Gardens, London SW11 7BW
A Penguin Random House Company

The authorised representative in the EEA is Dorling Kindersley
Verlag GmbH. Amulfstr. 124, 80636 Munich, Germany

10 9 8 7 6 5 4 3 2 1
001–327090–Jan/22

A CIP catalogue record for this book is available from the British Library.

ISBN: 978-0-24153-935-4
Printed and bound in the UK

For the curious
www.dk.com

This book was made with Forest Stewardship Council™ certified paper - one small step in DK's commitment to a sustainable future. For more information go to www. dk.com/our-green-pledge

Acknowledgements
The publisher would like to thank the authors and consultants Andy Psarianos, Judy Hornigold, Adam Gifford and Dr Anne Hermanson.

The Castledown typeface has been used with permission from the Colophon Foundry.

Contents

Ruby Elliott Amira Charles Lulu Sam Oak Holly Ravi Emma Jacob Hannah

Counting in hundredths

Starter

Charles, Holly and Jacob are playing a game. A board is used to keep track of their points. Each square is equal to 1 point. The game ends when all 100 squares are full.

What fraction of the board has each child filled so far?

Example

Charles has filled .

He has filled 1 hundredth of the board.

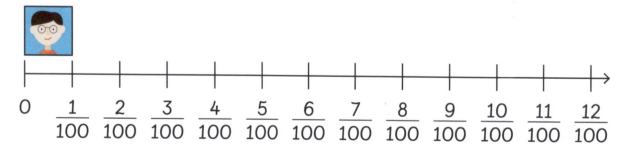

Charles has filled $\frac{1}{100}$ of the board.

Holly has filled  .

She has filled 7 hundredths of the board.

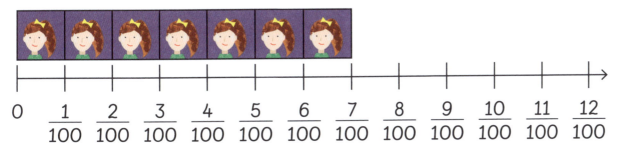

$$\frac{1}{100} \quad \frac{2}{100} \quad \frac{3}{100} \quad \frac{4}{100} \quad \frac{5}{100} \quad \frac{6}{100} \quad \frac{7}{100} \quad \frac{8}{100} \quad \frac{9}{100} \quad \frac{10}{100} \quad \frac{11}{100} \quad \frac{12}{100}$$

Holly has filled $\frac{7}{100}$ of the board.

Jacob has filled  .

He has filled 11 hundredths of the board.

Jacob has filled $\frac{11}{100}$ of the board.

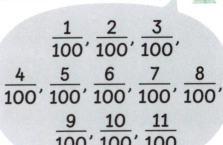

$$\frac{1}{100}, \ \frac{2}{100}, \ \frac{3}{100},$$
$$\frac{4}{100}, \ \frac{5}{100}, \ \frac{6}{100}, \ \frac{7}{100}, \ \frac{8}{100},$$
$$\frac{9}{100}, \ \frac{10}{100}, \ \frac{11}{100}$$

Practice

1   What fraction of each board is shaded?

(a)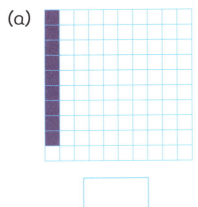

$$\frac{\boxed{}}{100}$$

(b)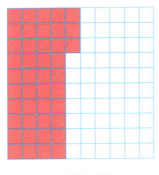

$$\frac{\boxed{}}{100}$$

(c)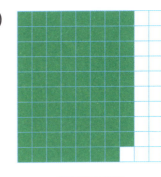

$$\frac{\boxed{}}{100}$$

2   Fill in the blanks on the number line.

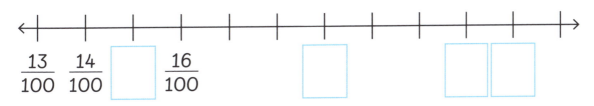

$$\frac{13}{100} \quad \frac{14}{100} \quad \boxed{} \quad \frac{16}{100} \quad \qquad \boxed{} \qquad \boxed{} \ \boxed{}$$

5

Mixed numbers

Starter

How many sandwiches are on the tray?

Example

   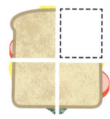

 There are 3 whole sandwiches.

There is $\frac{3}{4}$ of a sandwich.

$3 + \frac{3}{4} = 3\frac{3}{4}$

 We can write 3 and 3 quarters like this.

There are $3\frac{3}{4}$ sandwiches on the tray.

$3\frac{3}{4}$ is a **mixed number**.

What mixed number is shown?

This is 1.

This is $\frac{2}{5}$.

When we put a fraction next to a whole number it means we add the two together.

$1 + \frac{2}{5} = 1\frac{2}{5}$

1 and 2 fifths is $1\frac{2}{5}$.

$1\frac{2}{5}$ is a mixed number.

When we write numbers and fractions together we call them a mixed number.

Count in fifths to find the number shown.

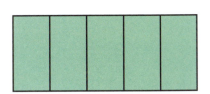 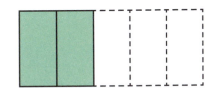

$\frac{1}{5}$, $\frac{2}{5}$, $\frac{3}{5}$, $\frac{4}{5}$, 1, $1\frac{1}{5}$, $1\frac{2}{5}$

1 How many brownies are there in total?

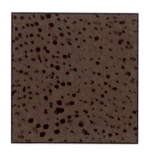  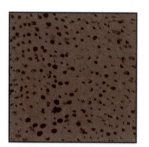 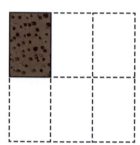

$$\boxed{} + \frac{\boxed{}}{\boxed{}} = \boxed{}\ \frac{\boxed{}}{\boxed{}}$$

There are $\boxed{}$ brownies in total.

2 How many rows of stamps are there altogether?

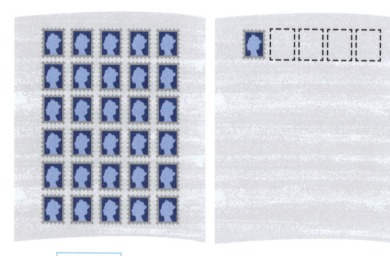

$$6 + \frac{\boxed{}}{\boxed{}} = \boxed{}$$

There are $\boxed{}$ rows of stamps altogether.

3 What are the mixed numbers being shown?

(a)

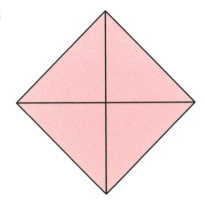

$2 + \dfrac{1}{4} =$ ☐

2 and 1 quarter is ☐ .

(b)

$1 + \dfrac{3}{10} =$ ☐

1 and 3 tenths is ☐ .

(c)

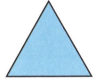

☐ $+ \dfrac{☐}{☐} =$ ☐

4 and ☐ thirds is ☐ .

Equivalent fractions

Starter

Is Jacob correct?

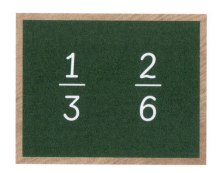

I think the numbers are equal.

Example

We can check if $\frac{1}{3}$ and $\frac{2}{6}$ are equal by using bar models.

I split this bar into 3 equal-sized pieces. Each part is $\frac{1}{3}$.

When $\frac{1}{3}$ becomes $\frac{2}{6}$, 1 larger part becomes 2 smaller parts.

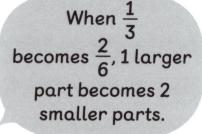

I split this bar into 6 equal-sized pieces. Each part is $\frac{1}{6}$.

$\frac{1}{3}$ is equal to $\frac{2}{6}$. They are equivalent fractions.

The bars show me that $\frac{1}{3}$ is equal to $\frac{2}{6}$.

Jacob is correct.

Are $\frac{1}{3}$, $\frac{2}{6}$ and $\frac{3}{9}$ equal?

$\frac{1}{3}$		

| $\frac{1}{6}$ | $\frac{1}{6}$ | | | | |

| $\frac{1}{9}$ | $\frac{1}{9}$ | $\frac{1}{9}$ | | | | | | |

I can see that $\frac{1}{3}$, $\frac{2}{6}$, and $\frac{3}{9}$ are all the same amount. They are equivalent fractions.

| $\frac{1}{5}$ | $\frac{1}{5}$ | $\frac{1}{5}$ | | |

| $\frac{1}{10}$ | $\frac{1}{10}$ | $\frac{1}{10}$ | $\frac{1}{10}$ | $\frac{1}{10}$ | $\frac{1}{10}$ | | | | |

| $\frac{1}{15}$ | $\frac{1}{15}$ | $\frac{1}{15}$ | $\frac{1}{15}$ | $\frac{1}{15}$ | $\frac{1}{15}$ | $\frac{1}{15}$ | $\frac{1}{15}$ | $\frac{1}{15}$ | | | | | | |

These are all equivalent fractions too.

$$\frac{3}{5} = \frac{6}{10} = \frac{9}{15}$$

Practice

Find the equivalent fractions.

1. $\frac{1}{7} = \dfrac{\boxed{}}{14} = \dfrac{3}{\boxed{}}$

2. $\frac{2}{7} = \dfrac{\boxed{}}{14} = \dfrac{6}{\boxed{}}$

3. $\frac{3}{10} = \dfrac{9}{\boxed{}} = \dfrac{12}{\boxed{}}$

4. $\frac{5}{9} = \dfrac{\boxed{}}{45} = \dfrac{50}{\boxed{}}$

Simplifying mixed numbers

Starter

Sam and Amira share 3 full boxes of chocolates.

 I take a full box and 4 chocolates.

I take a full box and 2 chocolates.

How many boxes of chocolates does each of them take?

Example

Sam takes 1 and 2 sixths boxes of chocolates.

 $1\frac{2}{6}$ can be simplified.

2 smaller parts become 1 larger part.

$$\frac{2}{6} = \frac{1}{3}$$

with $\div 2$ shown on top and $\div 2$ shown on bottom

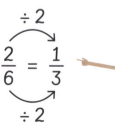

$1\frac{1}{3}$ is the simplest form.

Amira takes 1 and 4 sixths boxes of chocolates.

 chocolates

We can simplify $1\frac{4}{6}$.

$$\frac{4}{6} = \frac{2}{3}$$

$\div 2$ $\div 2$

4 smaller parts become 2 larger parts.

$1\frac{2}{3}$ is the simplest form.

Sam takes $1\frac{1}{3}$ boxes of chocolates and Ruby takes $1\frac{2}{3}$ boxes of chocolates.

Practice

1 Write each mixed number in its simplest form.

(a) $1\frac{4}{8} = \boxed{}$

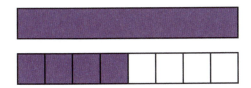

(b) $2\frac{3}{9} = \boxed{}$

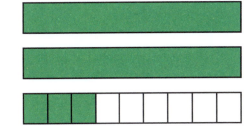

2 Simplify.

(a) $\frac{6}{8} = \dfrac{\boxed{}}{\boxed{}}$

(b) $\frac{8}{10} = \dfrac{\boxed{}}{\boxed{}}$

(c) $\frac{10}{12} = \dfrac{\boxed{}}{\boxed{}}$

(d) $3\frac{6}{9} = \boxed{}$

(e) $7\frac{4}{10} = \boxed{}$

(f) $9\frac{9}{12} = \boxed{}$

Adding fractions

Can you help the children solve these equations?

Example

$$\frac{4}{5} + \frac{1}{5} = \frac{5}{5}$$

If we add 1 fifth to 4 fifths we get 5 fifths.

$$\frac{4}{5} \quad + \quad \frac{1}{5} \quad = \quad \frac{5}{5}$$

5 fifths is equal to 1.

$$\frac{1}{7} \quad + \quad \frac{3}{7} \quad = \quad \frac{4}{7}$$

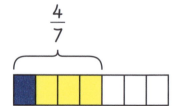

If we add 1 seventh to 3 sevenths we get 4 sevenths.

$$\frac{5}{9} \qquad + \qquad \frac{7}{9} \qquad = \qquad \frac{12}{9}$$

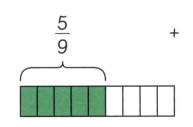
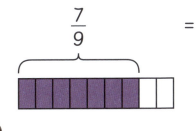

$$\frac{4}{5} + \frac{1}{5} = 1$$

$$\frac{1}{7} + \frac{3}{7} = \frac{4}{7}$$

$$\frac{5}{9} + \frac{7}{9} = 1\frac{3}{9}$$

5 ninths plus 7 ninths is equal to 12 ninths. 12 ninths is more than 1. We can simplify 12 ninths to 1 and 3 ninths.

Practice

1 Fill in the blanks.

(a)

☐ — ☐ + ☐ — ☐ = ☐ — ☐

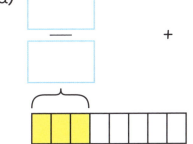
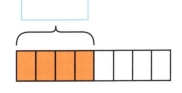
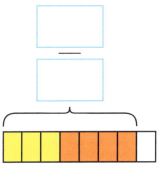

(b)

☐ — ☐ + ☐ — ☐ = ☐ ☐ — ☐

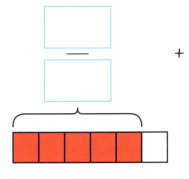
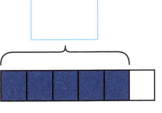
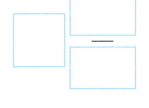

2 (a) $\dfrac{2}{7} + \dfrac{1}{7} = \dfrac{\Box}{\Box}$

(b) $\dfrac{2}{5} + \dfrac{3}{5} = \dfrac{\Box}{\Box} = \Box$

Subtracting fractions

Jacob puts $\frac{2}{9}$ of 1 tray of lasagne in a container.

How much lasagne is left?

Example

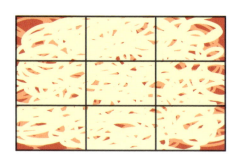

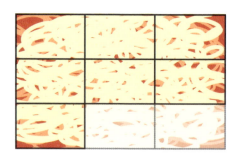

$1 = \frac{9}{9}$

Method 1

$2 - \frac{2}{9} = 1\frac{9}{9} - \frac{2}{9}$

$\qquad = 1\frac{7}{9}$

Method 2

$2 - \frac{2}{9} = \frac{18}{9} - \frac{2}{9}$

$\qquad = \frac{16}{9}$

$\frac{16}{9} = 1\frac{7}{9}$

There are $1\frac{7}{9}$ trays of lasagne left.

1 Subtract and fill in the blanks. Give your final answer as a mixed number.

(a)

$$2 - \frac{1}{5} = 1\frac{5}{5} - \frac{1}{5} = \boxed{}$$

(b)

$$3 - \frac{3}{7} = 2\frac{7}{7} - \frac{3}{7} = \boxed{}$$

(c) $8 - \dfrac{5}{9} = 7\dfrac{9}{9} - \dfrac{5}{9} = \boxed{}$

(d) $4 - \dfrac{1}{3} = \boxed{} - \boxed{} = \boxed{}$

2 Subtract and simplify the fraction.

(a) $4 - \dfrac{4}{10} = 3\dfrac{10}{10} - \dfrac{4}{10} = \boxed{}$

(b) $7 - \dfrac{6}{8} = 6\dfrac{8}{8} - \dfrac{6}{8} = \boxed{}$

3 Subtract and give your final answer as a mixed number.

(a) $2 - \dfrac{4}{5} = \dfrac{10}{5} - \dfrac{4}{5}$

$= \dfrac{6}{5}$

$= \boxed{}$

(b) $3 - \dfrac{5}{7} = \dfrac{21}{7} - \dfrac{5}{7}$

$= \boxed{}$

$= \boxed{}$

Adding and subtracting fractions

Starter

Elliott brings some pizza to the table.

Ruby takes $\frac{3}{5}$ of the pizza from Elliott.

How much pizza does Elliott have left?

Example

Find how much pizza Elliott has to start with.

1

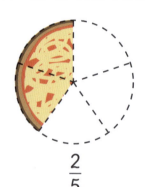

$\frac{2}{5}$

$1 + \frac{2}{5} = 1\frac{2}{5}$

Elliott had $1\frac{2}{5}$ pizzas.

Find the amount of pizza Elliott has left after Ruby took $\frac{3}{5}$ of the pizza.

1          $\frac{2}{5}$

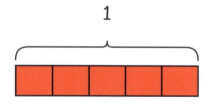

Subtract $\frac{3}{5}$ from $1\frac{2}{5}$.

$1\frac{2}{5} - \frac{3}{5} = \frac{7}{5} - \frac{3}{5}$

$\qquad = \frac{4}{5}$

Elliott has $\frac{4}{5}$ of the pizza left.

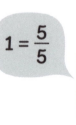

$1 = \frac{5}{5}$

18

1 There are $1\frac{1}{5}$ pepperoni pizzas. There is $\frac{2}{5}$ of a cheese pizza.

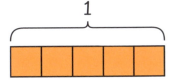  

If Jacob eats $\frac{4}{5}$ of the pizzas, how much pizza will be left altogether?

Add $1\frac{1}{5}$ and $\frac{2}{5}$.

$1\frac{1}{5} + \frac{2}{5} = \boxed{}$

Find the total amount of pizzas to start with.

Subtract $\frac{4}{5}$ from $1\frac{3}{5}$.

$1\frac{3}{5} - \frac{4}{5} = \frac{8}{5} - \frac{4}{5} = \boxed{}$

Subtract what Jacob eats from the total amount.

2 Emma has $\frac{4}{7}$ l of orange juice and $\frac{6}{7}$ l of apple juice.

She uses $\frac{5}{7}$ l of juice to make a smoothie.

What is the total amount of juice left after Emma makes the smoothie?

Find the total amount of juice. $\frac{4}{7} + \frac{6}{7} = \boxed{}$

Subtract $\frac{5}{7}$ l from the total amount of juice. $\boxed{} - \frac{5}{7} = \boxed{}$

There is $\boxed{}$ l of juice left after Emma makes the smoothie.

Fractions of lengths

Starter

Jacob and his friends go on a 16-mile bike ride.
After 30 minutes, they have cycled $\frac{1}{4}$ of the total distance.
How many more miles do they need to cycle?

Example

The entire bike ride is 16 miles. We need to find 1 quarter of 16.

If we split 16 into 4 equal parts, how much is each part?

We can divide to find out.
$16 \div 4 = 4$
Each part is 4 miles.

4	4	4	4

16

$\frac{1}{4}$ $\frac{3}{4}$

4	4	4	4

16

They need to cycle $\frac{3}{4}$ of 16 miles.
$\frac{3}{4}$ of 16 is 12.

Jacob and his friends need to cycle another 12 miles.

is characterised by massive rainfall between January and April, less so from October to November. Therefore, the days are hot and sultry with temperatures up to 40°C. The climate is more temperate along the coast and in the mountains. The winters are dry and daytime temperatures vary around 23°C. Regardless of season, the nights are chilly and the thermometer can drop to zero. The country is arid but the semi-desert type of weather provides regional variations. These disparities are linked to the local geography which has, in turn, required the wildlife and vegetation to adapt for survival in this harsh environment. Notwithstanding these rigours, Namibia has an unexpectedly prolific wildlife: 134 types of mammals; 620 of birds; 70 of reptiles; 20,000 of insects, amongst which are some of the world's rarest; 2,400 kinds of

flowering plants; and 345 grasses. These are just a few examples of the extraordinary dynamism of this captivating destination.

The Namib is an omnipresent, yet many faceted desert. For the purposes of this book, therefore, we have had to choose the most representative features from amongst its many aspects. So we will begin with the vistas of the giant Sossusvlei sea of dunes for which Namibia is most noted. Then we will linger for a while in the central region's mineral universe. After which we will return to the Skeleton Coast, which is renowned for its fur seals. Then we move across the chaotic topography of Damaraland to reach the red mountains of Kaokoland. At which point, we will end our itinerary in the celebrated but no less mythical Etosha National Park.

Even though the desert can present itself in many forms, the dunes remain the most telling symbol. Photographing them in the early or late hours of day helps you capture the most beautiful images, moments when the setting sun creates patterns of light and shade on the liquid sands. To take in such landscapes, a wide angle lens is recommended. The use of a polarising filter also helps to enrich the colours and achieves an even better result.

Namib Desert

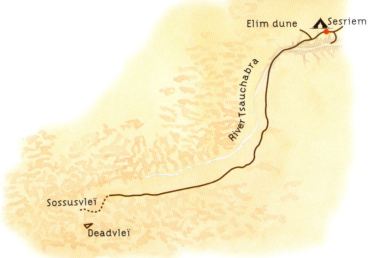

The formation of the Namib can be put at around 80 million years ago, which makes it the world's oldest desert. It occupies Namibia's entire Atlantic coastline from the Kunene River in the north to the Orange River in the south. As a result, the expansion of the desert is contained by these two waterways which wash its sands away towards the ocean. The Namib comprises two main environments: the sandy dunes that stretch along the coast of the Atlantic ocean and which cover an area of approximately 34,000 square kilometres – and inland, the rocky plains and high plateaux which represent about two-thirds of its territory. The Namibian Desert also accommodates the world's fourth, and Africa's biggest, national park, the Namib Naukluft, extending to 50,000 square kilometres. The ecology of this region, which has been protected since 1978, is complex. To understand better how the ecosystem functions, it helps to explain the influence the Benguela Current has on the dunes, and the remarkable adaptability of

In the dune lands, the presence of vegetation always seems incongruous; yet it is testimony to the incredible adaptability of plant life in even the most hostile of environments. But a subterranean source of water is never far away. Often, sand deposits build up around a plant until it disappears and forms another dune. The shapes and colours of shrubs can create interesting contrasts, especially with the sky and sand. For this type of shot, a medium focal length lens is preferable.

The shapes of the undulating sand dunes conform to factors that leave nothing to chance. As well as variations in wind speed and direction, the angle of the slopes is determined by the volume of available sand, the size and weight of individual sand grains and what other types of sand or gravel are present. Photographing just after daybreak, or shortly before sunset, gives the best light for a dramatic picture. Here the sun's rays are at ground-level and stress the relief of ripples sculpted by the wind. A wide angle lens will allow for the sweep of the scale of the landscape and a detailed foreground, and a polarising filter is again strongly recommended.

the fauna and flora, before exploring the majestic Sossusvlei. The Benguela current contains a mix of water from the Indian and South Atlantic Oceans that flows around the Cape of Good Hope. The prevailing winds blow offshore and cause cold rich water to upwell to the surface. This nutrient rich water generates exceptionally abundant marine life off the Namibian coast. It also has a fundamental influence on the desert ecology of the coastal zone. Being 6°C cooler than the ocean water offshore, the surface water readily evaporates, generating dense fogs which form at night. These fogs spread 50 kilometres – and in exceptional cases, up to 100 kilometres – inland, shrouding the central zone with an opaque veil that some days may not burn off until midday. This mist is a source of water for the specialised flora and fauna that exploit it. The cold ocean and hot continent create the desert conditions. This is why the fog – the region's only source of humidity – assumes significant biological importance for living organisms.

The Namib boasts unexpected wildlife, adapted to the worst of living conditions. Apart from insects, a few small mammals and some birds, the presence of reptiles is quite widespread on the slopes of the orange sands. To photograph the smallest of these, such as this lizard, a macro lens is necessary, along with a fair amount of patience.

It's not easy to climb a sand dune. It's often a case of one step forward and two steps back. But once at the top, views of the immense desert and its intoxicating silence are a great reward. Of course, a wide angle lens is recommended when trying to express this incredible sense of eternity.

In an ecosystem where water and nutrients are rare, the vegetation has had to develop efficient means of resisting the desert furnace and the parching assault of its winds. A typical example is the native nara melon which has adapted to escape the desert's harsh climate. Long roots dig deep into the sand in search of subterranean water tables, while surface foliage is minimised to limit the loss of moisture through evaporation. These fleshy shoots are widespread and much appreciated by ostriches, while the ripe fruit is enjoyed by many animals – notably gemsboks, jackals, brown hyenas, gerbils and porcupines. Other plants like the ganna assure their supply of water by absorbing the condensation deposited on their leaves whose surfaces dilate slightly to drink in the droplets.

With its lines and curves, an ocean of dunes can lend itself to endless visual essays. The photographer should linger awhile to experiment with all kinds of different foregrounds and lighting. Medium and long focal length lenses are ideal for capturing the patterns.

11

From the top of a dune, sunrise contributes even more intensely to the desert's magic spectacle. When its warm light floods the deafening silence, particles of dust glisten in the chilly morning air and emphasise the ephemeral contours being designed by another day. Only a telephoto lens allows you to record all the details of this magical moment.

The dollar bush, equally common in the dunes, also survives on underground water sources, and even though it takes care only to expose a single edge to the parching sun, its succulent round leaves sometimes exhibit obvious dehydration. Whether sited in the hot shade of a rock or exposed to the wind – the desert flora always beats a path towards water. This is collected by the extensive root system and stored in the fleshy stems and leaves. A leathery cuticle and thorns help to reduce water loss by evaporation – especially when the wind blows.

As with the vegetation, the survival of animals in the desert is a daily struggle for water. With the exception of the gemsboks the big species only frequent the burning hell

The gemsbok reigns over the desert as absolute master. No other animal equals its exceptional qualities for resisting the fatal heat of the sun. A sophisticated thermo-control system allows it to tolerate body temperature increases up to 45°C while keeping that of its brain at a lower level. This stems from a complex network of nasal blood vessels which cool the blood before it reaches the brain.

of the dunes on a seasonal basis. The native fauna is predominantly composed of insects, reptiles and rare small mammals. Although hard to see, by day they are always present, dependent upon a fragile food chain linked to the Benguela fog. Equally essential is the organic debris from plants and dead animals, that is carried on the wind. This debris helps to feed the desert creatures which must also be specifically acclimatised to the sweltering heat. The temperature at ground level sometimes reaches 70°C. Consequently, a number of animals like the golden mole spend the day buried in the sand and only come out when nightfall covers the dunes with its cloak of stars. Others, like the gecko, prefer thermal gymnastics. By jumping from one foot to the other, this amusing lizard avoids prolonged contact with the burning surface. If the temperature is too high, he joins his myopic neighbour in the relative coolness below ground or climbs to the top of a knoll to capture a breeze. Similarly, certain insects expose themselves to the wind in order to catch minute and vital water droplets on their shells. Apart from some beetles it can take a lot of time and patience to observe the activity of snakes, spiders, scarabs and other desert insects – inhabitants of a burning world of cruel light and heat.

The interest of these shots opposite is mostly in its composition. The foreground tree and dunes behind constitute the elements of a visual dialogue: the fragile survival of vegetation pitted against the invulnerability of the mineral world; the small irregular outline of one against the perfect and immense symmetry of the other; living matter with roots versus material that is unchanging yet moving. Together, they present a picture best taken with a medium focal length lens.

The desert presents a multitude of landscapes combining an endless palette of colours. Caressed by the sun, all these elements offer the photographer a wide range of picture compositions. The fluid, changing knolls – mauve or ochre depending on their natural lighting – reveal here and there a few patches of vegetation. Choice of lens here is unimportant provided you get the shot!

But before penetrating this ocean of dunes to explore its microcosms, Sesriem Canyon offers a beautiful walk through its labyrinth of flavescent rocks sculpted by the Tsauchab. The waters of the river only fill the narrow gorge during the rainy season, leaving a bed of sand in winter that is well suited to walkers wanting to explore the vegetation and discover the small animals that dwell in the shade of its cliffs. Some 60 kilometres towards the southwest, you come to the desert landscape of your dreams: Sossusvlei! The site has only been open to visitors since 1977 because initially it was part of a forbidden diamond field. Today, the classic image of these flowing mountains of sand is open to all. The giant dunes that undulate as far as the shimmering horizon are probably the world's highest with some attaining 300 metres. It is possible to climb them and contemplate a silent and velvety expanse where ochre, vermilion, pink and mauve blend harmoniously.

Each day, untiringly, the sunlight quietly reshapes the desert contours. In early morning or twilight, the sun is the best ally for the photographer who remembers to use a telephoto lens to tighten the angle of certain shots. Here, the narrow frame allows the perfect geometric lines to work, but also to isolate the light that plays on the sandy landscape.

Near Sossuvlei is the depression of Deadvlei. It is a basin of fine white clay surrounded by a jewel-case of ochre dunes. Long ago a forest appears to have occupied the site, but today – in stark contrast with their surroundings – only the black denuded tree trunks survive. Wide angle and medium focal length lenses are advised to explore all the photo possibilities offered by this unusual site, a place endowed with a somewhat strange and other-worldly mood.

In the event of an exceptional downfall, a temporary lake appears at the foot of the dunes. It becomes a meeting place for all of the desert's fauna including numerous birds, notably the avocet. Not far from here, like a dust volcano, is the Deadvlei Pan, set into the bottom of an orange sand crater, where the searing heat induces surreal images and hypnotic dreams. Five hundred years ago these acacia trees died after a sand barrier diverted the course of the Tsauchab River that periodically used to irrigate them. Charred by the sun, their black and gnarled trunks protrude from a base of cracked clay to create endless images of amazing beauty.

Namibia's originality stems from its vast expanses of desert and wilderness. Mountains extending to the distant horizon of huge plains are characteristic of central Namib where, as elsewhere in the country, the scenery varies at every turn. Finding a bit of height on a knoll or hill will allow you – with a wide angle lens – to combine foreground subjects with dramatic backgrounds.

Welwitschia Drive

Valley Moon

River Swakop

Husabberg
▲857 m

Langerheinrich
▲1152 m

Blutkoppe

Klein Tinka

Naukluft

The Naukluft forms part of the central Namib Desert. It is a region of bewitching charm where all the faces of the desert are apparent through a subtle chain of metamorphosis. Linear but changeable dunes, vast stony expanses and granite hills — embossing here and there a landscape littered with parched grasses — are among the Namib's most beautiful pieces of mosaic. One of this region's most spectacular locations is, without any doubt, the canyon of the Kuiseb River. Forming a natural border between the sea of dunes in the south and the rocky plains in the north, its waters only flow two or three times a year and its thin flow rarely reaches the ocean. The Kuiseb scoured its bed about 15 million years ago, but the accumulation of sediment forced it to open up a second bed, inside the former one. Today sand deposits again threaten to obstruct its course. The struggling riverside vegetation along its wide sandy bottom does not support or nourish significant wildlife. Because the canyon's waterholes are more numerous than downstream, numbers of kudu, zebra, springbok, klipspringer, jackal, chacma baboon and rock hyrax have all been spotted on various occasions. Less frequent and less predictable are appearances by leopard and spotted hyena.

The inselbergs – rocky boulders also known as kopjes – are frequent in the Naukluft region. In the early morning, when the sun embellishes the stone with its raw light, is the best time to enter this mineralogical chaos in the quest for new pictures. The wide vista calls for a wide angle lens, although a medium focal length is indispensable for highlighting details within this site.

Sparrows, like these red-billed queleas always gather at waterholes in colonies of hundreds. Their thirst quenched, they suddenly take off in a flurry of dull brown wings and untimely chirping. These birds are so small that a long focus lens is necessary in order to take in the flock but with the advantage of detailing certain individuals. But be careful, as it is not easy to take such a group shot. The answer is to trigger several shots per second. Use the same technique to photograph the spotted-backed weaver, looking for brushwood to make its nest.

caravan of panting gnus passing; where the tiny Damaraland dik-diks walk alongside the gracious black-faced impalas, both native to southern Africa; where brown hyenas, caracals and leopards leave only fleeting and mysterious traces of their nocturnal sorties; where the insect-eating bat-eared fox backs away from the cheeky jackal; where the kori bustard is almost as big as the steenbok. In short, it's probably the only park in the world where one can contemplate wildlife even at night, thanks to the floodlit waterholes close to each of the hospitality centres. The black rhinoceros — almost extinct and strictly protected — assiduously frequent these settings. In no way perturbed by the light, the animals come here without fear and provide a primitive spectacle of their elementary behaviour. That's how it is at Etosha.

When raindrops, like arrows, penetrate the earth's deep cracks, trees become adorned with tender green foliage that creates an unusual setting which wild birds jealously invade and occupy. Piercing the very pure air, as if rinsed by the rains, the violent morning sunlight heightens colour and contrast in this high definition portrait of a grey hornbill taken with a telephoto lens.

Practical information

LANGUAGES

English is spoken and understood by more than 10% of the population, however it may not be their language of choice. There are over 28 dialects in Namibia.

CURRENCY

Namibian dollar

ELECTRICITY

230/240 volt, round pins

LOCAL TIME

GMT +2 hours

WEATHER

Semi-desert with hot days and cold nights in winter from May to September; rainy season with high temperatures in summer from October to April.

LUGGAGE

Clothing: light items for daytime – short-sleeve shirts, T-shirts, bermudas, shorts; warm weather items for morning and evening especially in the desert – trousers, sweater or polar jacket, windbreaker. Footwear: a pair of good walking shoes and a light pair of shoes. Other items: hat, sunglasses, sunscreen (high index), anti-mosquito lotion, electric torch, personal first aid kit, passport, air ticket, credit card and debit card.

PHOTOGRAPHIC EQUIPMENT

Equipment: camera, lenses, tripod or monopod, flashgun, polarising filter (very useful for the Sossusvlei dunes), plenty of film or memory cards (for digital cameras), rechargeable batteries, normal batteries, power pack, dust-proof bag plus cleaning kit (brush and soft cloth), binoculars, bean bag (useful window stabiliser in vehicles) etc. Digital users will find a small external hard drive useful for downloading digital images. Photographers using film cameras, need to carry all films as hand luggage, to avoid fogging from the X-rays used for screening checked baggage.

ACCOMMODATION

Influenced by the historic presence of the Germans and the South Africans, Namibia is a very western country. This legacy is naturally reflected in the organisation of tourist hospitality. Hotels and restaurants – even modest ones – have little to learn from Europe. As for the camps, our preferred formula during our trip, they are located amidst very beautiful scenery but at very specific sites that are often closed. Sanitation here is pretty rudimentary and often non-existent. This means that tourist traffic is so sparse that finding a camp site is no problem. However, camping in the wilderness is not allowed. And at Etosha, where tourists are more numerous, you can forget about having the bush to yourself. There are three enclosed sites with bungalows, camp sites and restaurants that welcome visitors. No other choice is available. Happily, the wildlife spectacle compensates for these shortcomings. Furthermore, the Etosha camps all have waterholes (located outside the enclosure with observation decks). Floodlit at night, they allow wonderful viewing of the animals coming and going in complete freedom.

TRAVEL

Travel in Namibia is usually in a 4x4 vehicle because driving in sandy and rocky desert conditions always involves some risk. However, the main roads are excellent and well maintained with the exception of those in Kaokoland where, indeed these are none. But be careful not to drive off-road. Namibia's ecosystem is extremely fragile and the wheel marks left in the ground will remain carved in the ground for centuries. With few exceptions, vehicles are always enclosed and have no opening roofs. This is partly because of the constant presence of dust that infiltrates every nook and cranny. It is only during safaris – especially to Etosha – that the absence of an open roof is frustrating because you will have no choice but to photograph through windows. We have seen some operators put large lorries with canvas covers at the disposal of tourists, but these vehicles are not adapted to desert conditions and sand and dust get into everything. Nor are they well suited to safaris on account of being too big and frightening to animals and often too high to permit good angles for pictures. So make sure you inquire about local transport arrangements.

PARKS AND RESERVES

Wildlife conservation is enshrined in Namibia's very young constitution. Since the founding of the Etosha National Park in 1907, twenty other parks, nature reserves and tourist sites have been created to protect the country's extraordinary natural heritage. These ecologically-monitored spaces occupy about 13 per cent of national territory. Apart from Etosha, a dozen other parks account for most of this effort. They are: Daan Viljoen Game Park, Fish River Canyon National Park, Khaudom Game Reserve, Mahango Game Reserve, Mamili National Park, Mudumu National Park, Namib-Naukluft Park, Skeleton Coast Park and Wilderness, National West Coast Recreation Area, Waterberg Plateau Park and West Caprivi Game Reserve. Another 27 per cent of the country is totally uninhabited and remains the purest form of wilderness, notably certain parts of Kaokoland or Damaraland. The land configuration in these latter cases makes access almost impossible. Let us hope they remain preserved in their natural state.

Wildlife Photography

Exploring Namibia is not just another African safari, since wildlife is not the country's primary attraction. Namibia is, above all, a desert where grandiose scenery offers limitless opportunities to compose wonderful shots. The lines, the curves, the angles, the shapes and the colours offer the photographer an infinite treasure trove of creative ideas. Unlike animal photography, landscape shots give the photographer time to think and construct his composition. The principles of framing are the same and the light, as always, is best during the first and final hours of day. But be careful. In Namibia, the constant presence of dust and sand in the air filters the sunlight and dims its strength.

As for the lenses to take, the usual rules apply: a wide angle to embrace the immensity of the desert and allow for foreground; a medium focus of the 80-200mm zoom type to tighten the frame and to select particular parts of the scenery. A 300mm telephoto is also useful to highlight the lines and curves of the desert and create abstract figures, capture details, the texture and shapes of the ground. Finally, there's the extra long focus – probably the least indispensable for landscape photography – but much appreciated when highlighting the red disc of the sun at dawn on a distant mountain crest or on the horizon.

For animal photography in Etosha or the uplands of Damaraland and Kaokoland, long focus lenses such as the 400mm, 500mm or even 600mm are essential. They are, along with the 300mm, the most widely used telephoto lenses. Approaching wild animals is often difficult outside parks because they are shy and easily scared. While inside the parks it is compulsory to stay on the roads, the very place the animals tend to avoid. In Etosha, the animals gather particularly around waterholes that are generally within a reasonable distance of parking spots. For those interested in night shots, it is imperative to equip oneself with a tripod and strong flash to photograph the numerous species that crowd around the man-made pools near the Etosha camps. The rare black rhinoceros is frequently there, too. As always on safari, it seems to us that two camera bodies are a minimum requirement, especially when using different film speeds. Even though with a digital camera the ISO setting can be changed at anytime, two bodies are still recommended. This is because when photographing fast moving animals it is quicker to pick up another body with a different lens than spend time changing lenses and thereby miss out on the action.

Unlike the vehicles used in East Africa or the rest of southern Africa, most of those available in Namibia are not ideal for animal photography because they lack sun roofs so it is important not to forget the indispensable bean bag. Three-quarters full and positioned on a window shelf, it assures a stable base for telephoto shots and even those taken in weak light conditions. The waterhole and off-road aspects of Etosha do not help the photographer because the shooting angles are dictated by the availability of parking. So the challenge is greater. But be reassured that something always happens in the animal world and that these minor constraints have never prevented the great professionals from taking excellent shots.

As in all things, patience and determination are important virtues for a photographer, whether amateur or professional. It's mostly a matter of knowing how to wait and avoiding being discouraged when things fail to work out. Photography is a choice between a recorded document and an act of creation. Only individual sensitivity makes the difference and nature is sufficiently generous to allow self-expression. Some prefer to photograph a plant because it is rare, even if it is not photogenic, or an animal even if the sun is too bright. Others seek to extract from what they see the most harmonious and best-lit elements in order to compose a shot that is unique to them. In either case, it is good to be attentive and curious to find the best way to link wildlife reality to photographic imagination...